Original title:
Snow Angels and Hearth Flames

Copyright © 2024 Creative Arts Management OÜ
All rights reserved.

Author: Benjamin Caldwell
ISBN HARDBACK: 978-9916-94-422-6
ISBN PAPERBACK: 978-9916-94-423-3

Enchanted by the Chill

The whispering winds begin to sway,
As autumn leaves dance in their play.
A blanket of frost coats the ground,
In this quiet magic, peace is found.

The moon shines bright in a velvet sky,
Casting shadows where dreams drift by.
Each breath a cloud in the crisp night air,
Nature's silence, a spell we share.

The stars twinkle like diamonds up high,
While owls call softly, like a lullaby.
In every corner, the stillness thrives,
Amidst the chill, the heart revives.

With every step on the icy floor,
The world transforms, a mystic lore.
So let us wander, hand in hand,
In this enchanted, frosty land.

Woven in Winter's Light

In the hush of falling snow,
Silent whispers softly glow.
Branches cloaked in crystal sheen,
Winter's magic, pure and keen.

Footsteps crunch on icy ground,
Nature's breath, a tranquil sound.
Wrapped in blankets, hearts ignite,
Woven closely, spirits bright.

Twilight's Warm Caress

As the sun bows to the night,
Colors blend in soft twilight.
Gentle breezes kiss the trees,
Carrying secrets on the breeze.

Stars awaken, twinkling clear,
Drawing closer, night draws near.
In that calm, our dreams reside,
Twilight's warmth, our souls confide.

Murmurs Beneath the Stars

Underneath the vast expanse,
Silent wishes, hearts in trance.
Moonlight dances on the sea,
Whispers shared, just you and me.

Constellations weave their tales,
In the night, our love prevails.
Murmurs blend with evening's breath,
In this moment, life and death.

Frosted Illusions and Fiery Hearts

Amidst the chill, our spirits rise,
Frosted dreams beneath the skies.
Hearts ablaze with passion's fire,
In the cold, we find desire.

Whispers stir in winter's grasp,
Holding tight, we will not clasp.
Illusions dance like drifting snow,
Fiery hearts, an endless glow.

A Tapestry of Warmth and Wandering

In the glow of amber light,
Footsteps dance through shadows bright,
A tapestry of laughter spun,
Underneath the setting sun.

Wanderers with dreams in tow,
Seek the warmth of hearth and glow,
Stars above begin to gleam,
Filling hearts with hope and dream.

Frosty Blankets and Hearthside Tales

Outside the world wears white attire,
Inside, the crackling wood and fire,
Blankets wrapped, we gather near,
Sharing tales that warm the sphere.

Frosty patterns on the pane,
As we reminisce of joys and pain,
Each story woven in the air,
Binding us with love and care.

Winter Whispers

Whispers dance on winter's breath,
Silent echoes of life and death,
Frozen branches reach and sway,
In the quiet dusk of day.

Moonlight kisses glistening snow,
Flickers of warmth begin to glow,
As shadows stretch, the night unfolds,
Ancient secrets quietly told.

Frosted Wings of Grace

On frosted wings, the moments glide,
Into the stillness, hearts abide,
Graceful whispers touch the ground,
In the silence, peace is found.

Through crystal vistas, we may roam,
Each flake a story, each drift a home,
With every breath, the magic sways,
In winter's calm, our spirits blaze.

A Warmth Like No Other

In the glow of the firelight, so bright,
Comfort wraps around like a soft night,
Laughter echoes, hearts share,
A moment caught, blissful and rare.

Through the windows, winter's chill bites,
But within these walls, love ignites,
Pumpkin spice and cocoa's sweet scent,
Every breath a gift, every smile a moment spent.

As shadows dance on the wall's embrace,
We hold memories close, in this sacred space,
The world fades away, just you and me,
In a warmth like no other, we are free.

Snowflakes and Hearthside Tales

Outside, snowflakes fall and twirl,
Silent whispers, a winter swirl,
Inside, the hearth's familiar glow,
Tells of stories long ago.

With every crackle, a tale begins,
Of brave adventures, lost and wins,
A family gathered, hearts unfold,
In the warmth of love, there's treasure untold.

Mugs brimmed high with sweet delight,
Fingers warming in the soft twilight,
Together, we share the tales we weave,
In snowflakes and warmth, we believe.

Chasing the Soft Light

The sun dips low, a gentle sigh,
Colors paint the evening sky,
We chase the light that fades away,
Embracing hope in the twilight's play.

Footsteps whisper on the cool ground,
With every heartbeat, magic is found,
A fleeting moment, a shared glance,
In the soft light, we take a chance.

As day surrenders to night's embrace,
We find our dreams in this sacred space,
Together we navigate shadows' flight,
Chasing the beauty of soft, fading light.

Wings of Whimsy and Warmth

In a garden where daisies sway,
Imagination takes its flight today,
With wings of whimsy, bright and true,
We dance through dreams, just me and you.

The air is filled with laughter's tune,
Under the gaze of a silver moon,
Hearts ignite like stars in the night,
In this softness, everything feels right.

Let's wander far where magic creeps,
In corners where the wild heart leaps,
With every flutter, love finds its path,
On wings of warmth, we embrace the aftermath.

Beneath the Frosty Canopy

In the quiet of the night,
Snowflakes dance, a gentle sight.
Branches draped in winter's lace,
Whisper secrets in this place.

Stars above in silence gleam,
Nature's hush, a tranquil dream.
Underneath this frosty dome,
Hearts find warmth, a fragile home.

Hearts Ignited in Winter's Breath

Chilled winds blow, yet fires blaze,
In our souls, the warmth stays.
Together we face the frost,
In each other, we are not lost.

Snowflakes fall, the world aglow,
In our hearts, a steady flow.
Winter's breath may chill the air,
But love's warmth is always there.

White Feathered Dreams

Softly drifting through the air,
Feathers light without a care.
Dreams take flight on wings so white,
Guided by the silver night.

In this realm of pure delight,
Every glance and every sight.
Whispers of the night's embrace,
Feathered dreams, a sacred space.

Glowing Shelters of Solace

In the woods, a cabin stands,
Firelight flickers, warmth expands.
Within these walls, we find our peace,
Moments shared that never cease.

Glowing comforts, soft and bright,
Wrap us warmly through the night.
Outside, winter sings its tune,
Inside, hearts hum a soft rune.

Warmth Beneath the Icy Veil

Underneath the cold, we hide,
Where whispers of warmth coincide.
Soft echoes of laughter blend,
With memories that will not end.

In shadowed corners, hearts ignite,
Holding close through the winter's night.
The frost may bite with chilling grace,
Yet warmth resides in our embrace.

Flurries of Love in Ember's Dance

Gentle snowflakes swirl and sway,
Each one a word we long to say.
In the silence, passion glows,
As a fire's warmth within us grows.

Embers flicker, casting light,
On dreams that shine through the night.
Holding hands, we twirl and play,
In love's embrace, we'll find our way.

Frost-Kissed Dreams and Glow of Home

The night's embrace is crisp and bright,
While dreams take flight in gentle light.
Frost-kissed windows frame our view,
Of starlit skies and love so true.

Within these walls, a hearth aglow,
Binds us close with warmth we know.
Silent moments, soft and sweet,
In our haven, love's heartbeat.

Elysian Forms in White Haze

In the hush of winter's clutch,
Elysian forms unfold as such.
A veil of white, serene and bright,
Brings forth dreams in pure delight.

Amidst the haze, we find our peace,
As frigid winds begin to cease.
Hearts entwined in snowy bliss,
Serenity found in a silent kiss.

Luminous Spirits on a Frosty Canvas

Beneath the stars, the night unfolds,
A frosty breath where silence holds.
Luminous whispers dance on high,
As spirits twinkle in the sky.

The canvas glows with colors bright,
In cold embrace, they share their light.
Each shimmer tells a tale of old,
In frozen dreams, their stories told.

As dawn approaches, hues refine,
A magical brush of the divine.
Nature's palette still remains,
In hearts of those who hear the strains.

With every breath, the morning breaks,
A symphony that softly wakes.
The luminous spirits fade away,
Yet linger in our hearts to stay.

The Stillness of a Warm Embrace

In quiet corners, love resides,
A tender touch where time abides.
The stillness wraps the world in peace,
As gentle hearts find their release.

Beneath the warmth of twilight's glow,
Each whispered secret starts to flow.
Embraced by comfort, shadows blend,
With every heartbeat, love transcends.

In moments shared, we find our place,
A refuge carved in soft embrace.
Where silence speaks in tender tones,
And joy is felt in heart's own moans.

As night descends with velvet grace,
We linger long in this embrace.
For in this stillness, we belong,
Our love, a quiet, soulful song.

Radiance and Chill in Perfect Harmony

Under the moon, a chill prevails,
Yet warmth emerges in hidden trails.
Radiance dances, soft and bright,
In perfect harmony with the night.

The crisp air wraps around our skin,
In every breath, new life begins.
Radiant stars, like diamonds spread,
In chilly silence, all is said.

Footsteps echo on frosty ground,
In the stillness, beauty found.
Each moment shared, a fleeting spark,
Radiance glowing in the dark.

Together, we chase the ephemeral,
In radiance, our hearts are literal.
Chill and warmth, a soothing blend,
In perfect harmony, love transcends.

Delicate Whispers of the Frostbound Night

In frosty air, soft whispers flow,
Like secret dreams in moonlight's glow.
Delicate shadows dance and weave,
A tapestry that we believe.

The night unfolds with gentle grace,
Each breath a promise, time won't erase.
Whispers caress the silent trees,
As night itself begins to tease.

Crystals form in the silver light,
A beauty veiled, yet ever bright.
Delicate echoes in the still,
A symphony of heart and will.

As dawn peeks over hills so wide,
These whispers fight to stay inside.
Yet in our hearts, they'll ever stay,
In frostbound dreams, they find their way.

Whispers in the Winter Light

Softly falls the snow tonight,
Whispers dance in silver light,
Every flake a secret shared,
Carried gently, hearts ensnared.

In the hush, time drifts away,
Underneath the moon's soft sway,
Footsteps leave a fleeting trace,
As we wander, lost in grace.

Branches bare, but tales unfold,
In this quilt of white, we're told,
Nature's breath, a subtle art,
Whispers warm the winter's heart.

Embers of a Frosted Night

Embers glow in twilight's stir,
While frost glistens like a blur,
Silent stars begin their show,
Dancing softly, pure and slow.

Crackling firesides, warmth bestowed,
Each flicker writes a story owed,
With every spark, a dream ignites,
In the stillness of the nights.

Wrapped in blankets, hearts alight,
Chasing shadows, holding tight,
Embers whisper tales of old,
In the frost, the warmth unfolds.

Chasing the Chill of Fire's Glow

As the winds begin to wail,
We gather close, our dreams set sail,
Chasing warmth in flickering flames,
In the night, we call their names.

Each ember's dance, a fleeting thought,
In the quiet, wisdom sought,
Through the chill, our spirits rise,
Finding solace, 'neath the skies.

Fingers brush against the light,
In this haven, hearts unite,
Chasing chill, we find our flow,
Bound together, fire's glow.

Celestial Wings on Frozen Ground

Underneath the starlit vault,
Whispers of the night exalt,
Celestial wings take gentle flight,
Guiding dreams beyond the night.

Frozen ground beneath our feet,
Each step echoes, soft and sweet,
In this realm, where shadows play,
Hope ignites the cool decay.

With every breath, the cosmos calls,
In the silence, magic sprawls,
Celestial dance, a moment found,
As we weave through frozen ground.

Echoes of the Hearth

The fire crackles, warm and bright,
As shadows dance in the fading light.
Whispers of stories, old and wise,
Gathered together beneath the skies.

Faces glow in the flickering flame,
Each one remembered, none the same.
Laughter echoes, filling the air,
In this haven, we lose our cares.

Comfort found in the smallest things,
The joy of friends and what it brings.
In the heart, these moments stay,
Echoes of love, never fade away.

Footsteps in the Silent White

Blankets of snow, soft under foot,
Silent whispers as we stroll, mute.
Footprints linger on a frosty trail,
   Each step forward tells a tale.

Branches heavy with winter's grace,
Nature's beauty in this silent space.
Chill in the air, yet warmth we find,
   In every step, the heart aligned.

The world sleeps beneath a shimmering sheet,
   In the stillness, our hearts gently beat.
With every breath, a moment to share,
   In this frozen realm, a love affair.

Cinders and Crystal

In the fading light, embers glow,
Cinders dance, with a life of their own.
Crystal shards glimmer in the night,
Reflecting tales of warmth and fright.

Memories linger, wrapped in flame,
Each spark a whisper, calling a name.
Time's gentle hand holds us near,
In flickers of hope, we conquer fear.

The heart's fire, though dimmed with time,
Burns with a truth, a silent chime.
Amongst the ashes, dreams still rise,
Cinders and crystal under the skies.

Enchantment Under the Frozen Canopy

Where branches meet in a frosty embrace,
Magic lingers in this hidden place.
Snowflakes twirl, a dance so divine,
Under the canopy, stories entwine.

Whispers of winter fill the trees,
Carried softly on a chilling breeze.
Darkness blankets the world outside,
Yet here, the heart ignites with pride.

Hope sparkles like stars on a clear night,
In frozen wonder, all feels right.
With every breath, enchantment flows,
In this secret realm, true love grows.

Whispers of the Evening Glow

The sun sinks low, a golden kiss,
A tender hush, the world's sweet bliss.
Shadows dance where twilight plays,
In whispers soft, the evening stays.

Stars emerge, their secrets told,
A tapestry of night unfolds.
Moonlight weaves through branches bare,
While dreams take flight upon the air.

Crickets sing in harmony,
Nature's symphony, wild and free.
The gentle breeze, a lover's sigh,
Beneath the vast, enchanting sky.

In this moment, time stands still,
The heart finds peace, the soul we thrill.
With every breath, the night aglow,
In whispers soft, the evening's flow.

Glacial Epiphanies

In winter's grip, the world stands still,
A crystal coat on valley's hill.
Breath becomes mist, a fleeting trace,
In icy realms, we find our space.

Mountains rise, their peaks so high,
Reflecting dreams against the sky.
Silent moments, thoughts unfurl,
In frozen frames, we pause and twirl.

The day retreats, a fading light,
While shadows stretch into the night.
With each soft crunch beneath our feet,
We dance with frost, a tender beat.

In glacial grace, truth finds a way,
Shattering silence, here we stay.
Moments glimmer, cold and bright,
Epiphanies burn through the night.

Flickering Hopes in the Frost

Amidst the chill of winter's breath,
Flickers of light defy the death.
Each tiny flame, a story told,
In warmth we gather, hearts unfold.

Snowflakes swirl in soft ballet,
Each one a wish, a hopeful sway.
As candles flicker, spirits rise,
In every glow, a sacrifice.

Whispers of warmth in the cold night,
Mirrored dreams of flickering light.
Hope rests gently in the frost,
In every flame, no love is lost.

We hold these moments, dear and tight,
Flickering hopes, our guiding light.
Together we face the winter's chill,
In the dance of shadows, our hearts still.

Tapestry of the Hearth's Glow

Around the fire, tales are spun,
A tapestry where hearts are won.
The warmth envelops, stories blend,
In every heartbeat, love transcends.

Embers dance with a golden hue,
Carving memories, old and new.
Laughter echoes, shadows play,
In the hearth's glow, we find our way.

The flicker bright, a beacon's call,
Uniting souls, we rise or fall.
With open arms and tender gaze,
We cherish moments, love ablaze.

In this cocoon, we find our peace,
The world outside feels like release.
Together woven, hand in hand,
In the hearth's glow, forever stand.

Chasing Shadows in the Snow

Footprints fade in winter's glow,
Whispers of a tale untold.
Every flake a silent throw,
Dreams in white begin to unfold.

Trees stand tall, draped in frost,
Echoes of laughter fill the air.
In the quiet, we feel the lost,
Chasing shadows everywhere.

A glimmer of light flickers near,
Guiding us through the chill of night.
With each step, we cast aside fear,
In this world, everything feels right.

Snowflakes dance like secrets shared,
Memories captured in the freeze.
In the stillness, hearts bared,
Chasing shadows, chasing peace.

The Dance of Light in the Dark

Amidst the night, the stars will play,
Flickering whispers, soft and bright.
A ballet of dreams in the gray,
Guiding us through velvet light.

Moonbeams pirouette with grace,
Creating patterns on the ground.
In this space, we find our place,
Where silence speaks without a sound.

Shadows blend in a fleeting grace,
Each moment a snapshot of bliss.
In darkness, we embrace the chase,
For light's a tender, timeless kiss.

As dawn awakens, the dance subsides,
Yet memories twinkle in the sky.
In our hearts, the magic resides,
A gentle spark that will not die.

Beneath the Glittering Tapestry

Underneath a jeweled dome,
The cosmos whispers tales of old.
Every star a piece of home,
Woven into myths retold.

Galaxies spin with stories bright,
In the quiet, secrets sigh.
Painting dreams in colors light,
Where wishes take their flight.

Threads of silver, strands of gold,
Connecting hearts across the night.
In the vastness, we unfold,
Beneath the glowing, endless light.

Holding onto this celestial grace,
We find our place in the design.
As stardust dances, time will trace,
A forever bond, yours and mine.

Whimsy in a Winter Wonderland

Snowflakes twirl like laughter's sound,
Blanketing the world in white.
Every corner, joy is found,
In this magical winter night.

Children's voices fill the air,
Building dreams with every snowman.
In the chill, we have not a care,
Wandering freely, hand in hand.

Twinkling lights in every tree,
Adding sparkle to the scene.
In this wonder, we are free,
Living moments pure and serene.

As shadows stretch and day gives way,
Whimsy wraps us in its glow.
In winter's heart, we find our play,
Creating magic through the snow.

Candlelight and Glacial Grace

Flickers dance on walls of night,
Whispers breathe in soft delight.
A warm embrace, a gentle hue,
In shadows deep, the heart stays true.

Frosty breath on windows gleams,
As candle wax drips down in streams.
Each flame a story, quietly told,
Of love and warmth when night is cold.

A flicker bright, a faint retreat,
Where darkness lingers, secrets meet.
In glacial grace, the world slows down,
While candlelight paints the town.

Embrace the glow, let worries fade,
In this moment, memories made.
The world outside may chill and bite,
But here we find our own warm light.

Wrapped in Winter's Soft Caress

Snowflakes fall like whispers sweet,
Blanketing earth with a hush so neat.
Pines wear white in steady grace,
A beautiful world, a silent space.

The air holds crisp, a joyful bite,
As daylight dims and stars ignite.
Wrapped in winter, a tender close,
Nature rests, and soft wind blows.

Hot cocoa warms the chilly hands,
As laughter sings in quiet bands.
Friends gather close, by the fire's glow,
Wrapped in winter, love will flow.

In this stillness, time stands still,
Hearts are light, and dreams fulfill.
Each moment gleams, a treasure found,
In winter's arms, we're always bound.

The Lure of the Fire's Glow

Crackling whispers, the fire's song,
Pulls us close, where we belong.
A dance of shadows on the wall,
In the warmth, we find it all.

Flickers cast in amber light,
Stories shared in the velvet night.
A spark ignites the evening's tale,
As embers glow and spirits sail.

As night falls deep, the world sleeps tight,
We linger here, hearts alight.
The lure of flames, a tender bind,
In the fire's glow, love intertwined.

With every spark, a wish will rise,
Beneath the vast and starlit skies.
Together, we savor each glowing show,
In the magic found in the fire's glow.

Shimmering Silence in the Night

Stars embrace the quiet air,
Each twinkle, whispers left to share.
Moonlight spills on fields of white,
In shimmering silence of the night.

Footsteps soft on powdery ground,
Where nature's peace is all around.
A world transformed in silver light,
Lost in dreams, we take our flight.

The trees stand still, a solemn guard,
In this crisp and enchanted yard.
Night's embrace is a gentle theme,
In silence, we weave our dreams.

Breathless moments, still and clear,
In this nocturnal atmosphere.
Together we wander, side by side,
In shimmering silence, we abide.

Flakes that Kiss the Ground

Softly they fall, a gentle dance,
Whispers of winter, a fleeting glance.
Each flake a wonder, unique in grace,
Covering earth in a pure embrace.

Children rejoice, with laughter and cheer,
Building their dreams, winter's frontier.
Snowmen arise, with coal for their eyes,
In a world transformed beneath silver skies.

Under the moon, they shimmer bright,
A blanket of diamonds in the night.
Cold winds may blow, yet hearts stay warm,
In the beauty of snow, we find our charm.

As morning breaks, a sunlit scene,
Sparkles of magic, fresh and serene.
Flakes that kiss, then quietly mend,
Nature's soft touch, on which we depend.

Flames that Cradle the Chill

In the hearth's glow, shadows play,
Dancing with whispers of passing day.
Embers flicker, a warm embrace,
Beneath the stars, we find our place.

Cold winds howl through the night's deep,
The fire's warmth wraps, lulling to sleep.
Stories are shared, hearts intertwine,
Around flickering flames, we sip our wine.

The logs crackle, with softest sighs,
Each ember a spark, as time gently flies.
In the chill outside, the heart's aglow,
With flames that cradle, our spirits grow.

Through winter's grasp, we gather near,
In the dance of fire, all doubts disappear.
With every flicker, our worries still,
Together we feel those flames that thrill.

Twilight's Serene Blanket

As the sun dips low, a hush fills the air,
Stars begin to twinkle, a celestial flare.
The horizon glows in shades of blue,
Wrapped in twilight, the world feels new.

Gentle whispers float on the breeze,
Nature's lullaby rustles the leaves.
Day bids farewell, while shadows play,
In twilight's embrace, we drift away.

Crickets chirp their evening song,
Under the cloak where we belong.
Golden hues fade to deeper tones,
In twilight's arms, we find our homes.

A moment suspended in soft twilight,
Where dreams awaken and worries take flight.
Serene and quiet, the world unwinds,
In this gentle time, peace we find.

Emberlight Dreams

In the stillness of night, softly they glow,
Embers of dreams that flicker and flow.
Whispers of visions, both near and far,
Lighting the path like a guiding star.

With every heartbeat, stories arise,
In the warmth of the fire, beneath midnight skies.
Hope's gentle flicker ignites from within,
Emberlight dreams where wonders begin.

As shadows deepen, the night takes hold,
Treasures of memory in stories untold.
Through the gentle curls of the drifting smoke,
We gather our dreams, as the embers bespoke.

So let us dream, wrapped in the night,
Where embers of warmth fill hearts with light.
In the soft hush of dark, let our spirits soar,
Emberlight dreams, forevermore.

The Dance of Cold and Warmth

In the heart of winter's chill,
A flicker of warmth begins to spill.
Snowflakes twirl in a glimmering light,
While fires crackle through the night.

Soft shadows dance on the icy ground,
Amidst the silence, warmth is found.
Cold breezes weave with embers bright,
Creating harmony in the night.

The frost and flame take turns to sway,
As day gives in to twilight's play.
Their waltz spins tales of sweet delight,
A balance crafted, cold and bright.

With every breath, a story told,
Of seasons met, both young and old.
In this embrace, they find their home,
The dance of cold and warmth, alone.

Silent Gardens of Crystal

In a garden where the snowflakes fall,
Every branch and leaf stands tall.
Crystal whispers in the air,
Silent wonders everywhere.

Each petal cloaked in frosty lace,
Nature's stillness, a gentle grace.
Amidst the hush, the world does gleam,
In frozen beauty, a waking dream.

Footsteps softly in the drifts,
As daylight through the branches lifts.
Silent gardens, a secret place,
Where silence holds a tender trace.

Underneath the veil of white,
Life awaits to reunite.
In thawing moments, hope resumes,
In gardens dressed in winter's blooms.

A Hearthside Reflection

By the hearth, where embers glow,
Memories dance in the fire's flow.
Each flicker tells a tale untold,
Of warmth and love in the bitter cold.

The crackling wood sings a song,
Of days gone by, where we belong.
In shadows cast, the stories spin,
Reflections of the heart within.

Faces gathered, laughter shared,
In every moment, we've declared,
That home is where the heart can stay,
By the hearthside, night turns to day.

With every spark, a wish takes flight,
In the cozy cradle of the night.
Here, we find our peace regained,
In the warm embrace of love unchained.

The Magic of Frozen Moments

In the stillness of a winter's day,
Frozen moments softly play.
Time stands still in icy grasp,
Memories caught in a crystal clasp.

Each breath forms a fleeting cloud,
In the quiet, clear and loud.
Glistening trees in the fading light,
Whisper secrets of the night.

Snowflakes twinkle, a fleeting bliss,
Each one crafted, a perfect kiss.
In their fall, the world can dream,
Of magic found in winter's gleam.

With every step on the frozen ground,
Echoes of magic all around.
These moments linger, hearts entwine,
In winter's spell, we find the divine.

Wings of Winter's Muse

Soft whispers of the cold,
With dreams in layers, unfold.
Snowflakes dance on the breeze,
Nature's art, a tranquil tease.

In silence, echoes abound,
In every flake, beauty found.
The sky wraps in a soft quilt,
Where hopes and warmth are built.

Moonlight glimmers on the frost,
In stillness, nothing is lost.
Each moment, a silent sigh,
Beneath the vast, embracing sky.

With each step, a story spun,
The journey's just begun.
In hollow trees, secrets wait,
Winter's muse, a timeless fate.

Flickering Aspirations

Stars that blink in darkened skies,
Hopes rise up, as the morning cries.
In the depths of quiet night,
Dreams ignite with flickering light.

Through shadows cast by doubt's hand,
We seek out a brighter land.
Each flicker, a whisper of fate,
Guiding hearts toward the great.

Embers glow with a warming gleam,
Awakening the fragile dream.
Together, we chase the dawn,
With aspirations reborn.

In torrents of the fleeting night,
We gather strength, we gather light.
With every breath, courage swells,
Flickering joy, the heart compels.

When Frost Meets Flame

A dance of cold and warmth entwined,
In every touch, a bond defined.
Frost kisses fire, a fleeting grace,
In this clash, we find our place.

Crackling whispers fill the air,
As heat and chill become a pair.
Moments freeze in blazing glow,
Time suspends, the world below.

Colors swirl in twilight's embrace,
Mirrored souls in a warm space.
With each flicker, stories take flight,
When frost meets flame, day meets night.

Hearts will battle, yet inspire,
In every struggle, we acquire.
This union bold, both fierce and sweet,
Together, they create the heat.

Lullabies in Glistening White

Blankets soft, the earth in dreams,
Underneath the moonlight beams.
Whispers sing through evergreens,
Lullabies in silver scenes.

Gentle coats of purest snow,
Wrap the world in a lovely glow.
Each branch bows with a tender weight,
Nature rocks us, calm and great.

In the hush, the heart finds peace,
In the silence, worries cease.
Beneath the stars, we lay so light,
Cradled in this glistening white.

As the night enfolds us tight,
Embrace the calm, the soft respite.
In these moments, tender, bright,
Find your dreams in endless flight.

Flames that Ignite the Heart's Retreat

In shadows deep, embers glow bright,
Whispers of love in the coldest night.
Flickering voices, secrets untold,
Warmth from the heart, a fire to hold.

In silence we gather, our spirits entwined,
A dance of the flames, the sparks combined.
Echoes of laughter, as flames rise high,
In the heart's retreat, we soar and fly.

Together we stand, against the fierce wind,
Each flicker a promise, each glow a friend.
Through darkened paths, our light will guide,
In flames that ignite, let our hearts collide.

With every heartbeat, a pulse of desire,
Fueled by the passion, we build our fire.
A sanctuary found, where souls can meet,
In the heart's retreat, love's flame, so sweet.

Winter's Breath and Fire's Embrace

Chill in the air, a whispering sigh,
Nature wraps us, beneath the gray sky.
Yet inside the hearth, the firelight gleams,
Filling our hearts, igniting our dreams.

Snowflakes dance, in the softest flight,
Each twist a story, pure and bright.
But here in the warmth, we feel so alive,
Under winter's breath, together we thrive.

The crackle of wood, a soothing sound,
In fire's embrace, our souls unbound.
Holding each other through the long night,
In flickering shadows, we find our light.

Two hearts together, against the cold's might,
Fueled by the warmth, in the soft, amber light.
Winter may linger, but here we will stay,
In love's gentle glow, we'll find our way.

Ethereal Shapes in the Silent Snow

White blankets flow, across the still ground,
Whispers of silence, a beauty profound.
Each flake a story, unique in its fall,
Painting the world, a canvas for all.

Shapes of the night, in the moon's soft glow,
Forms that enchant, as the cold winds blow.
Ghostly shadows move, in the cold, crisp air,
Ethereal shapes, a vision so rare.

Footsteps muffled, in this tranquil scene,
In snow's soft embrace, like a lingering dream.
Under the stars, with hearts open wide,
In silence, we wander, side by side.

Memories weave through the frostbitten night,
In beauty, we find our hearts take flight.
Ethereal shapes give life to the glow,
In the heart of winter, we learn to flow.

Heartbeats Beneath the Winter Sky

Stars shimmer bright, in the crisp, cool air,
Each heart that beats, a rhythm we share.
Beneath the vast sky, dreams take their flight,
In the stillness of winter, we feel the light.

Footprints in snow, a story to tell,
Of laughter and love, as we cast our spell.
Adventures await, in the cold silver night,
Together we journey, with souls intertwined.

From dusk until dawn, we embrace the chill,
With breaths visible, we climb every hill.
In whispers and glances, a bond that we weave,
Beneath the winter sky, we truly believe.

Heartbeats echo, as the night whispers low,
In the warmth of your hand, I'll never let go.
Woven like starlight, our dreams together lie,
In the magic of winter, beneath a vast sky.

Warmth in the Chill

In the quiet, the fire glows bright,
Casting shadows that flicker at night.
A blanket wraps tight, a hug to hold,
Against winter's grasp, a heart made bold.

Steam rises gently from mugs we share,
With whispers of dreams that linger in air.
Snowflakes dance softly on window panes,
While laughter echoes, as joy remains.

Warmth of togetherness lights up our souls,
In this season of cold, the spirit consoles.
Fireside tales spun with love and glee,
Creating memories, just you and me.

Dances of Ice and Ember

In twilight's glow, the embers spark,
While outside sings the wind's cold lark.
Dancing flames like grace in flight,
In contrast to the freezing night.

Frost clings tight to branches bare,
While warmth embraces without a care.
Two worlds collide, a stunning sight,
As ice and ember unite in light.

Against the chill, we find our way,
In the dance of fire, we choose to stay.
Together we laugh, together we dream,
In the glow of warmth, we potently beam.

Celestial Air and Glowing Hearth

The stars above in velvet spread,
Whispering secrets of the day long dead.
Beneath this sky, we gather near,
With the hearth aglow, casting out fear.

The air is crisp, each breath a song,
As we huddle together where we belong.
The universe twinkles, a distant grace,
While here on earth, we find our place.

Tales of wonder near the warm flame,
With hearts aglow, we're never the same.
Celestial air fills our dreams each night,
With the hearth keeping us snug and tight.

The Quiet Embrace of December

December's hush blankets the land,
As snowflakes drift, so soft, so grand.
In peaceful moments, time stands still,
With winter's breath, the world we fill.

Frosty mornings kissed by the sun,
Wrap us in stillness, our hearts are one.
The quiet embrace, a tender sigh,
As nature sleeps beneath the sky.

Fires crackle in gentle glow,
Binding us close as whispers flow.
In December's arms, we find our grace,
In the quiet, we carve out our space.

Flickers of Joy against the Cold

In the chill of winter's breath,
Tiny lights begin to glow.
Each spark a promise of warmth,
Chasing shadows, melting snow.

Hearts ignite with laughter bright,
Moments shared beneath the stars.
A flicker here, a dance of light,
Healing wounds, mending scars.

As snowflakes twirl, we hold tight,
Hand in hand, we face the night.
With each spark, our spirits rise,
Flickers of joy fill the skies.

In the dark, we're never alone,
Each smile a beacon, a gentle tone.
Embraced in love, we find our way,
Flickers of joy keep cold at bay.

Warm Breath in a Cold Embrace

Beneath the frost, a whisper lies,
A warm breath in the frozen air.
It dances softly, a sweet surprise,
Breaking through the winter's snare.

In tangled branches, truths unfold,
Memories wrapped in a cozy haze.
With every step, the warmth I hold,
Shimmers bright in twilight's gaze.

The chill may bite, but hearts collide,
Creating warmth that knows no bounds.
In each embrace, love will abide,
Softening the harshest sounds.

Together we breathe, a tender song,
In cold embrace, we gladly belong.
With every sigh, the world feels right,
Warm breath glowing through the night.

Glowing Memories of Warmth

In corners where the shadows play,
Ghostly whispers of laughter remain.
Flickers of warmth from yesterday,
Embracing us within their chain.

Christmas lights and stories told,
Around the fire, joy would bloom.
Memories wrapped in hues of gold,
In the heart, they chase the gloom.

Each glowing tale, a treasured thread,
We weave through time, a tapestry.
In every smile, the past is fed,
Holding close what we can see.

As winter falls with softest grace,
Glowing memories find their place.
In the silent nights of old,
Warmth is found in stories told.

Frosted Dreams of Yesteryears

In the stillness of winter's breath,
Frosted dreams come out to play.
They whisper tales of love and depth,
Echoing from a distant day.

Each flake a memory, crisp and bright,
Dancing down from skies of gray.
They paint the world in soft, pure light,
Revealing shadows of yesterday.

We walk through time on icy paths,
Holding dreams like fragile glass.
With each step, the past, it laughs,
Reminding us of moments passed.

Frosted dreams, like a gentle sigh,
Comfort the heart, make spirits fly.
In the cold, they weave and twirl,
A tapestry of life unfurl.

Dancing Shadows in the Quiet White

In the hush of falling snow,
Shadows sway to whispers low.
Moonlight finds a crystal stage,
Stars ignite the winter's page.

Footprints trace a fleeting tale,
Where the night winds gently wail.
Underneath the silver sky,
Dreams take flight, and spirits sigh.

Snowflakes twirl, a graceful dance,
In their motion, hearts entranced.
Each breath meets the frosty air,
In this trance, we linger there.

Through the night, the shadows play,
Guiding hope along the way.
As the dawn begins to break,
In their light, a world awake.

Gentle Flickers Amidst the Blanking Frost

Fires crackle, soft and bright,
Flickers born from silent night.
Each glow a whispered memory,
Holding warmth in reverie.

Outside, the frost claims every leaf,
Nature dons its stark motif.
Yet inside, the hearts ignite,
Gathered close, we chase the night.

Stories shared in hushed delight,
Laughter dances, taking flight.
Through the chill, our spirits soar,
Gentle warmth forevermore.

In the glow, we find our song,
United here, we all belong.
Beyond the frost, the world awaits,
In our hearts, love never waits.

Memories Kindled in the Winter Glow

By the fire, memories bloom,
Kindled softly, dispelling gloom.
Faces lined with tales of old,
In the warmth, our hearts unfold.

Snowflakes drift like whispered dreams,
Tales of laughter, woven seams.
Glimmers of a childhood's cheer,
In the glow, we hold them near.

Evenings rich with cocoa's scent,
Moments cherished, love's content.
Time slows down, each heartbeat flows,
In the hush of winter's throes.

Every glow a cherished spark,
Wrapping us in perfect arc.
Memories kindled from the past,
In this glow, forever cast.

Petals of Light on a Frozen Path

Along the trail where shadows linger,
Petals dance with light's soft finger.
In the stillness, visions play,
Guided by the break of day.

Frosted edges grace each bloom,
Carrying whispers, dispelling gloom.
Walking on this crystal thread,
With each step, our hopes are fed.

Nature's art upon the ground,
In the silence, beauty found.
Footfalls echo, soft and true,
As we wander, me and you.

Petals shine like stars anew,
In this dance of love, we grew.
On this path, our spirits soar,
In the light, we are once more.

Glimmers of Heat in a Crisp World

Whispers of warmth in the breeze,
Sunrise paints the frosty trees.
A dance of shadows, light on snow,
Hearts aglow in nature's show.

Footsteps crunch on icy ground,
Chasing dreams where warmth is found.
A flicker bright beneath the frost,
Moments cherished, never lost.

Hope emerges as daylight breaks,
Each breath clouds, yet warmth awakes.
In the chill, our spirits rise,
Glimmers shining in the skies.

Beneath the frozen, life is hid,
In every crack, a flame is bid.
Crisp world holds a secret treasure,
In the cold, we find our pleasure.

Celestial Patterns in Frigid Air

Stars align in velvet night,
Frigid air, a tranquil sight.
Constellations dance so free,
Whispers of eternity.

Moonlit paths in frosted hue,
Silent tales of me and you.
Each sparkle tells a story bright,
In the chill, we find our light.

Patterns weave in the heavens high,
Crystals glisten, as nights fly by.
A cosmic quilt in midnight's glare,
Celestial secrets fill the air.

As winter holds its breath so still,
Hearts ignite with steadfast will.
In the cold, our spirits soar,
Celestial dreams forevermore.

Surrendering to the Warmth Within

Close your eyes and feel the glow,
Let the warmth in, let it flow.
Beneath the layers, fire burns bright,
In quiet moments, find your light.

Embrace the comfort of each breath,
In the stillness, conquer death.
Hold the warmth that softly grows,
In the heart, the love bestows.

With every heartbeat, let it rise,
An inner sun, no need for skies.
Surrender to the heat inside,
Let it shine, let it abide.

In the dark, let shadows fade,
Where warmth exists, no fears invade.
Together we ignite the spark,
Surrendered souls, against the dark.

The Spark of Life Beneath the Chill

In icy realms, a warmth persists,
A flicker found in the cold's midst.
Underneath the frozen crust,
Life weaves dreams, in hope we trust.

Beneath the snow, the roots entwine,
Silent whispers in the pine.
Every flake, a story told,
Of life reborn, of hearts that hold.

In the chill, a pulse remains,
A gentle push, through winter's chains.
Each breath witnessed, a sacred time,
In frozen air, we still can climb.

The spark ignites as spring draws near,
From frozen soil, we shed our fear.
In every frost, a tale unfurls,
Life still pulses in winter's pearls.

Dreams Drenched in Frostlight

Silent whispers in the night,
Under stars that gleam so bright.
Cold winds carry secret sighs,
Where the frozen dreams arise.

Moonlit paths of silver frost,
In the quiet, worlds embossed.
Every flake a tale untold,
In the chill, our hearts grow bold.

Glistening in the morning haze,
Nature's art in frozen gaze.
Frostlight wraps the earth anew,
Painting skies in lavender hue.

In this realm of tranquil grace,
Time slows down, a gentle pace.
Lost in dreams, where hopes ignite,
Drenched in magic, pure and bright.

Hushed Symphony of Winter Nights

In the stillness, shadows creep,
Snowflakes dance and angels weep.
Pine trees sway with quiet breath,
Cloaked in white, they hide their death.

Stars awaken, gleaming high,
In the void of velvet sky.
A symphony that nature plays,
Echoes soft in frosty ways.

Every corner whispers tales,
Of hidden paths, and icy trails.
In this hush, the world lies still,
Cradled by a gentle chill.

Crystals form on window panes,
Framing dreams in icy chains.
Through the night, the silence sings,
In this peace, the heart takes wings.

Embrace of Light and Chill

Morning breaks with golden beams,
Warming all our frozen dreams.
In the air, a frosted bite,
Embracing both the warmth and light.

Chill winds whisper through the trees,
Softly dancing with the breeze.
Clouds drift slowly, white and bright,
Holding magic, day and night.

In this blend of cold and warm,
Nature finds her perfect form.
Every moment feels divine,
In the merge where soft hearts shine.

As suns set, the shadows grow,
Painting landscapes in a glow.
Embrace the chill, embrace the light,
Together they create delight.

Shimmering Reflections

Ripples dance on crystal lakes,
Mirrored skies in still heartaches.
Every breath, a whispered dream,
In the silence, secrets gleam.

Shadows waltz where sunlight plays,
Chasing echoes of the days.
Glimmers flicker, soft and rare,
Painting stories in the air.

Through the night, reflections shine,
Twinkling like celestial wine.
Water's edge, a canvas bright,
Where reality meets the light.

In the dawn, as waters flow,
Nature weaves her gentle show.
Shimmering, the moments last,
In reflections, futures cast.

Celestial Caresses

In twilight's grace, the stars align,
Soft whispers drift through gentle pine.
Moonlit dances on silver streams,
Eternal night, where magic gleams.

Robins sing, the dawn awakes,
Each note cradles what the heart makes.
Celestial threads weave through the air,
Carrying dreams beyond compare.

The cosmos twirls in cosmic glow,
Galaxies shimmer, secrets bestow.
In every heartbeat, the universe sighs,
A symphony written in endless skies.

With every breath, the night unfolds,
Stories told by starlight bold.
Celestial caresses, pure delight,
In the arms of the deep, serene night.

Hearthside Echoes of Warmth

Flickering flames cast shadows bright,
Stories weave in the soft candlelight.
Close-knit laughter, memories shared,
In comfort's cradle, love is bared.

Blankets wrapped in a cozy embrace,
Fireside whispers, a tranquil space.
The aroma of spices fills the air,
Every moment cherished with tender care.

Time slows down as embers glow,
Hearts connect in the hearth's warm flow.
Echoes linger, a melodic tune,
Under the watch of the silvery moon.

Seasons may change, but here we stay,
Amidst the warmth of love's array.
In hearthside echoes, life feels right,
Wrapped in the magic of the night.

Frosty Veils and Searing Hearts

Beneath the frost, a silence wounds,
Whispers carried through icy hues.
Veils of winter, a chilling grace,
Yet warmth ignites in a secret place.

Snowflakes dance, a fleeting glance,
Hearts in turmoil, lost in the trance.
Amidst the cold, passions ignite,
Frosty veils can't dim the light.

Longing eyes meet in quiet despair,
In the heart's furnace, flames lay bare.
Through winter's grasp, love perseveres,
Searing hearts conquer frostbitten fears.

So let the chill weave its icy song,
For love's embrace will ever be strong.
In frosty veils, our spirits soar,
Searing hearts, forevermore.

Glimmers Through Winter's Gaze

Amidst the grey, a flicker glows,
Hope emerges where cold wind blows.
Glimmers dance on each snowy crest,
Whispers of warmth in winter's vest.

Through frosted glass, the world seems still,
Yet beneath the surface, life's will.
Each spark a promise, bright and true,
Revealing paths of dreams anew.

In silence, the heart learns to roam,
Finding glimmers that guide it home.
Winter's gaze can chill the bone,
But within it dwells a strength unknown.

So as the snow blankets all it sees,
Remember the warmth found in the breeze.
Glimmers through winter's gaze ignite,
A radiant glow in the darkest night.

Warm Shadows Linger in the Cold

In twilight's grasp, the shadows play,
Flickering soft as dusk turns gray.
Chilled whispers cling to every wall,
While warmth retreats, yet we remain tall.

Through frosted panes, a glow appears,
A hearth's embrace as night draws near.
We gather close, the world outside,
In warm shadows, our hearts abide.

The winter's breath, a silent vow,
In cozy corners, time allows.
We share our dreams, our hopes unfold,
As warm shadows linger in the cold.

Outside, the world wears icy lace,
But inside blooms a gentle space.
With every laugh, and every sigh,
Warm shadows dance as moments fly.

Echoes of Laughter in the Icy Stillness

Beneath the hush of frosty eves,
Echoes stir where laughter weaves.
In icy stillness, voices blend,
With warmth that echoes, hearts transcend.

Snowflakes fall like whispered dreams,
In twilight's grasp, the quiet gleams.
Each chuckle echoes through the night,
A tapestry of pure delight.

Windows glow with candle's light,
Shadows dance, a lovely sight.
As laughter rings, our spirits soar,
In icy stillness, we want more.

Through frosted void, our joy breaks free,
In every chuckle, unity.
Though winter wraps the world in white,
Echoes of laughter bring us light.

Ethereal Visions in the Hearth's Breath

In the hearth's breath, warmth unfolds,
Ethereal visions, stories told.
Flames that flicker, shapes that sway,
In dancing light, our dreams convey.

Soft embers glow like stars at night,
Casting a spell, a gentle light.
In every flicker, memories weave,
Through shadows deep, our hearts believe.

The world outside draped in cold,
Yet here within, warmth takes hold.
In ethereal whispers, hopes arise,
Beneath the watchful, starlit skies.

Here in the calm of night's embrace,
Ethereal visions find their place.
While the hearth breathes, we gather near,
In radiant warmth, we have no fear.

Dreamscapes on a Blazing Sky

As daylight fades, the colors burst,
Dreamscapes weave, a vibrant thirst.
In blazing hues, the sky ignites,
Painting dreams in sweet delights.

Brushstrokes soft on canvas wide,
With every sunset, worlds collide.
The whispers of dusk call us near,
In vivid visions, hearts find cheer.

Each twilight glimpse, a fleeting chance,
In blazing sky, our spirits dance.
With dreams alight, we chase the night,
On dreamscapes bright, our hopes take flight.

With every star that lights the dome,
In blazing sky, we feel at home.
So let the dreams like fireflies fly,
In the night's embrace, we aim high.

Frostbound Reverie

In the stillness of the night,
Whispers dance on crystal air,
Moonlight glimmers, softly bright,
Nature's breath, a frozen flair.

Trees adorned in glistening white,
Silent dreams in winter's hold,
Stars wrapped tight in velvet night,
A blanket soft, a tale untold.

Footprints trace the endless path,
Echoes in the silent ground,
Gentle sigh of winter's wrath,
A reverie where peace is found.

Frosty breath upon the glass,
Sketches made by time's soft hand,
Moments pass, like fleeting grass,
In this realm, we understand.

Illuminated Moments of Bliss

Sunrise spills in hues so bright,
Colors bursting, hearts awake,
Gentle whispers of delight,
In each breath, the joy we make.

Laughter floats on warming breeze,
Tickling leaves, the sun's embrace,
In this dance, our spirits seize,
Every moment finds its place.

A single touch, a knowing glance,
Frames of life in fleeting light,
Every heartbeat fuels the chance,
To savor all, the purest sight.

Once in shadows, now we shine,
Woven threads of joy so true,
In these moments, hearts align,
Illuminated, me and you.

The Softness of Winter's Touch

Gentle flakes begin to fall,
Whispers from the icy skies,
Nature's quilt, a soothing call,
Blanketing the world in sighs.

Branches bend in tender grace,
Holding crystals, jewels rare,
In this hush, a sacred space,
Winter's kiss, a lover's care.

Fireplaces crackle, glow,
Stories shared on chilly nights,
With each ember's warm and slow,
Hearts are kindled, dreams in flight.

Breathless moments caught in chill,
Softened edges, time stands still,
In winter's arms, we find our way,
The softness of a snowy day.

Hearthside Stories Wrapped in Warmth

Fires crackle, shadows sway,
Echoes of the past unfold,
In the warmth, we find our way,
Hearthside stories gently told.

Comfort blankets piled high,
Laughter spills like sweetened tea,
Weaving dreams that never die,
In this space, we're truly free.

Eyes alight with tales of old,
Memories wrapped in soft embrace,
Each word a treasure, a bit of gold,
Sharing moments, time can't erase.

Outside whispers winter's chill,
Inside burns a love so bright,
Hearthside stories, hearts can fill,
Wrapped in warmth, we share the light.

Milton Keynes UK
Ingram Content Group UK Ltd.
UKHW022050111124
451035UK00014B/1043

9 789916 944233